C000117012

Zone

Zone

Poems of the Bosnian War

Stuart Laycock

Zone
published in the United Kingdom in 2015

by Leslie Bell trading as Mica Press
47 Belle Vue Road, Wivenhoe, Colchester, Essex CO7 9LD
www.micapress.co.uk | books@micapress.co.uk

ISBN 978-1-869848-04-0
First Edition

ACKNOWLEDGEMENT
Grammar was published in The Canterbury Festival Poet of the Year
2015 Anthology as Bosnia Grammar

Contents

I went into Bosnia on aid missions seven times during the war of 1992-1995. My visits were spread over a number of years and across a range of destinations. I also returned to Bosnia on aid missions a few times after the war. Some of these poems I wrote at around the time of the war, some I wrote recently after I watched, for the first time, films I took during the war and shortly after it. Watching the films was almost like being there again, and I have written some of the later poems, like some of the earlier poems, in the present tense.

Dedicated to those aid workers who each did far more to help in Bosnia-Herzegovina than I did or ever could have done and particularly to Tony and Neil, killed near Sarajevo, 1995.

We have to go
through Tuzla,
ten minutes' drive distant.
But the Dutch UN sergeant,
looking almost apologetic,
says Tuzla is being shelled.
He shrugs and speaks,
'Wait and see, maybe in an hour.
Have a cup of coffee.'
Somebody sniffs. Others shrug.
Tony lights up a cigarette.
We go and find a pool table
in the Dutch bar,
frenetic Euro-techno playing.
I pick to play stripes.
In the corner sits a
battered sculpture of Tito.
On his head he wears
a toy peach-coloured cowboy hat.

The siege has gone
but peace has not yet come.

A few days ago the
last sssssshell fell
on this side of Mostar's river.
But the snipers
are not yet redundant,
still putting in the odd, lazy
appearance at work.

No one yet is moving
the rows of grey, rusting
school lockers that lock your shadow
safe from the telescopic sights.
Few stop to admire the view
from the bouncy rope bridge
while taking a chance
for water.

The upstairs wing of the hospital
has been hit heavily,
rooms with gaping holes
that let in sunlight and lead.
The downstairs is thick with smells,
with grey limbs and faces
hiding camouflaged (too late)
against the grit grey blankets.

Pointing at their wounds
'Sniper', 'Sniper', 'Sniper',
they shout, grinning
in apologetic pain and glee at us.
One face reaches for a grin
but manages just a smile,
her right breast mashed by shrapnel.

Even in the brave spring sunlight
faces are pale from too long
in cover. Bodies are thinner
from too little food for too long,
but the defiant red lipstick
on girls' mouths is strong
and a smile is met
and held.

The war has done a thorough job
on this part of town, a real,
career-committed job of demolition.
Few buildings are unwounded,
ugly shell splat marks
(scars the shape of paint
splashed from upturned cans)
pock the road like misplaced acne.

The minarets on two of the mosques
are amputees
and the Stari Most (old bridge)
that embraced both banks of the city
and saw young boy friends leap to impress
has followed them to the resting place
of Mostar's love and girlish laughter
locked in the turquoise of the
sad Neretva.

DON'T MEAN

Those who live,
ache for death
to have meaning.

To be not so transparent,
but opaque with
impressively twisted
strands of sense.

When supersonic metal
slashes and carves, surely, we hope,
it must sculpt some great purpose
and we will nod our heads wisely
and say 'Now we see.

Now we understand
why it had to be like this.
We did not know our destination
when we began this journey
but now we have arrived
and the effort
was worthwhile.'

Could we cope
if the grimy suspicion grabbed us
grubby with frontline dirt,
reaching from the soil
like a bony hand
partly skin-covered,

that death don't mean anything.

GONE

The speed sign
still warns us
to slow down
for a village
where no village
exists any more.

Each and every house
is burnt, destroyed,
gone, kicked over
by the war boots
of the last three years.

A charming country village,
in life each little house
was different,
this cottage with a vine trellis,
that house surrounded by
a white fence.
In death, it is almost the same.

But the corpse of every
house lies slightly differently,
this untouched except for
the burnt roof gone,
and white walls
black at the edges,

that half-crumbled,
with a dirty green carpet
hanging suicidally
from a now gaping bedroom,
wardrobe doors swinging open
to show abandoned clothes.

If one single house,
just one, still lived,
big or small

(it wouldn't matter which)
then death would
not be absolute,
the pain not half so dark.

STOPS

1912, 1914, 1941, 1991, 1998.

This is where the 20th century stops
where it slumps into piled earth grave
wooden marker post thrust
stake-like into its vampire heart.

This is where the 20th century stops
empty windows smiling black
from burned buildings
and gap-toothed empty doorways

This is where the 20th century stops
individuals thrown from individual homes
into hunched collectivity
on roads aflower with steel-scraped scars

This is where the bloodiest century stops
where it also all bloody began
on a road in the Balkans
heavy with history and death.

BRIDGE

You still soar, fly in old photos, old prints
a pure arc, cloud white
above the turquoise Neretva,
a tourist dream of baked stone
afloat on hazy summer heat.

Maybe you thought
your days of history were done,
a well-earned retirement beckoned,
smiling, experienced, for tourists
and local lovers in the twilight.

But then came the war.
I was here in Mostar, in early 93,
could have met you,
felt your stones beneath my feet,
but I was busy in another part of town.

You did not wait.
I watched the grainy film of your death,
you shuddering, falling to your knees,
then sliding gracefully into the depths,
always graceful you even in death.

And now I visit
your carcass, months too late,
your smashed stumps
reach out to nowhere,
but they have strung a little footpath
between, little wires of hope,
little cables carrying life,
a zombie bridge maybe,
but still flying.

GRAMMAR

The thump smashed the air,
the cloud of dust billowed
lazily, lethally, climbing the sky.

'Who is shelling whom?' you asked.
Quite right. Never let a little thing
like war murder grammar.

USED

Shameful to say,
after seeing so many,
you get sort of used
to houses that have been
merely burned.
Homes emptied of life
and roasted by flame,
blackened roof beams
scratching the sky,
roof tiles swivelled at impossible angles,
or crinch crunch
smashed on the floor.

A few shrapnel scars,
or bullet holes,
on walls can add interest,
gouge marks that tell
of a building's death.
Or even projectile holes
punched round through a wall
as if somebody had a rifle
big enough to kill a house,
tearing brick skin and mushing innards.

But still, but still
one thing never loses
the power to shock.
When houses have been
not burned right down
but blown right up.
When a house, a home,
is left a metre tall,
concrete on flattened concrete,
like dough under a giant's fist.
Fee fi, fo, flat.

HAPPY

They tell me
some experts
when asked
why God allows evil
say how could we
enjoy the good
if we never
experience the bad?

I don't buy that
but there again
lying here
in a hot bath
with you sat beside it
and cold wine in my hand
back from the Bosnian snow
and the mud and the sadness
I've never been so happy
and may never be
ever again.

TONY

We did our best, Tony.
Honest we did.

A few months after
you and I shared
a truck cab to Tuzla,
we were sharing
a truck cab again,
only this time
you, ashes in an urn.

They wanted you
scattered in Bosnia
where you died
helping the people.
So we did that.

Wasn't quite how
I imagined it.
The war was moving
a bit fast by then,
artillery in the wild hills.

So we left you
at peace I hope,
despite the booms
in the background,
on a spur
behind the hospital.

Prayers in the air
and Last Post on a harmonica.
Yep, not quite what
a hero deserves,
but we meant it.

Rest in peace, Tony.

Know

They don't get disposable
nappies here very often.
Well, it's the war,
of course,
you know.

But when you're
running a hospital for doubly
incontinent disabled kids
it's tough,
you know.

Using old clothes
tucked in to soak up
the piss and rest, well that
ain't much fun,
you know.

Particularly when most of
your washing machines
have broken down and
can't be mended
you know.

So if the stench
gets just too bad
well vomiting
wouldn't be good
so we'll just breathe through
our mouths,
you know.

War to the south of us
war to the north of us
war, a lot of war, to the east of us
but in Split it's Spring.

People stride in the Adriatic light
sunshine clothes on,
no mud, no camouflage.
A pretty girl smiles at me,
maybe thinks my camcorder
makes me TV crew.

People chat,
flowers grin red from baskets
and the only history is
Rome's emperor Diocletian
who first built the place,
so long ago that all
his wars and his troops
are just words on a page.

Amidst the fruit and the flowers
a little stall does sell tacky,
metal war badges,
but you don't have to stop,
and the hotels on the outskirts
are full of refugees
but not here.

Here, on the sea-front
the tourist menus still offer it all,
in once lurid now fading photos
(though you might be best
not to expect it all).
And the war seems
a million miles distant,
until a UN helicopter
grey white against the

cyan sky briefly disturbs
the Spring chatter.

But soon the interruption is gone.
God, I love this place

SARAJEVO CAT

The cat abandoned its doze
and went and looked through the shellhole.
It gingerly wrinkled its nose
and wondered who'd made such a hellhole.

PARK

The park's not quite
what it used to be
but then that's war
for you. Mucks everything up.

Before it all started,
lovers would walk arm in arm,
as the dusk descended,
and listen to cicadas grunt.

A girl's laughter split the air,
a flick of hair,
she smoothed it behind her ear.
Footsteps soft on the gravel.

Somewhere a radio played,
music lifted on the warm air of
summer and men's laughter
low and satisfied drifted from a café.

Now the flowers rest in vases
and lovers rest in the earth.
Fading wooden headboards
spell out the names of the gone.

Helmets hang on some
of the markers
and an empty shell case
stands vertical, sad sentinel.

With a bit of mental arithmetic
you can get the age
from the dates. 19, 22, 24, 20,
then, oh look an old one, 50.

But the cicadas are still here
and even though elsewhere
in Bosnia, they are digging graves,
they're carving none here.

At least, not today.

THE CAMP

(after Rosenberg, Returning, We Hear The Larks)

The night's dark
and burnt houses lurk beyond camp's wire
but we're OK, we've made it through another day.

We're tired and the trucks are knackered,
the road's shit and ankle-deep in mud
but the UN will let us get a little sleep.

And here in the middle of the chaos
oh, joy, they have food and drink
and phones to call England.

Somebody could drop a shell
on the base tonight,
but the only thing that does drop
is army canteen food on a plate,
sausages sweet as kisses,
chips hot as love.

YUGOSLAVIA

At home,
I have a book,
fading on a shelf
with a title that now seems
more threat than invitation –
Holiday Yugoslavia 1990.

Not sure if
Holiday Yugoslavia 1991
ever made it to the presses.
And Holiday Yugoslavia 1992
was never going to be
a best-seller
what with the war
and all.

Still, riveting reading,
Holiday Yugoslavia 1990,
telling of a world gone.
Where Gorazde is
recommended for fishing.
Where Mostar Bridge's death
makes no appearance.
Where Serbs, Croats and Bosniaks
get no mention.
Where the big new story on Sarajevo
is the 1984 Winter Olympics.
And where Srebrenica
isn't even in the index.

But beware, oh Traveller 1990.
Not for nothing
does the introduction
to the Bosnia chapter state
that the impact on world history
of this tiny region is
far, far bigger than its size.

FAT

Maybe one day
far in the future
I'll be fat and tired
and old and bald,
and then I'll think
of Bosnia
and I'll say to myself
actually we helped save
quite a few lives
and those lives
that we saved
went on to
have kids
and make more
little lives
who will go on
to produce more lives
and more and more
until the end of time,
like stars in the
night sky over the
Neretva gorge
stretching to infinity
and it'll all
feel so worthwhile
and I won't seem
quite so fat and old
and tired any more.

GREY

Sometimes everything
in the hospitals seems grey.
The sheets grey,
the blankets grey,
walls and ceilings grey,
bandages grey,
stretchers grey,
the faces of the patients grey,
the beard shadows on wounded
soldiers grey,
eyes silent with resignation grey,
the windows grey,
the sky outside grey.
Even when they have colour
they're still all grey.

CORNER

You don't have
to be young to die
in a war like this.
No age discrimination here.
You don't have
to be male,
you don't
have to be fit.
The war's happy
to take you nonetheless.
In the corner,
past the young men
staring silently at the
bandaged stumps
where their feet
or a hand had once been
an old lady who had
never worn camouflage,
not in this war at least,
lay dying,
bleeding to death,
quietly.
She'll be gone now.

Destroyed bridge and pontoon bridge, Neretva gorge

Pakistani UN armoured cars patrolling road in northern Bosnia, 1995

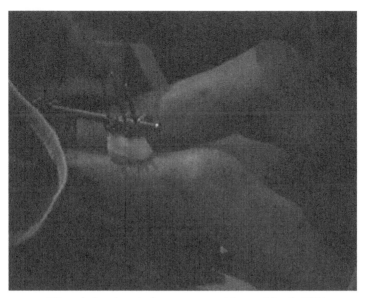

Wounded patient in basement east Mostar, March 1994

Bosnian soldiers, central Bosnia, 1994

23

Wrecked house in Gornji Vakuf, 1994.

Sign in Gornji Vakuf.

Gun crew near Gornji Vakuf, 7th March 1994.

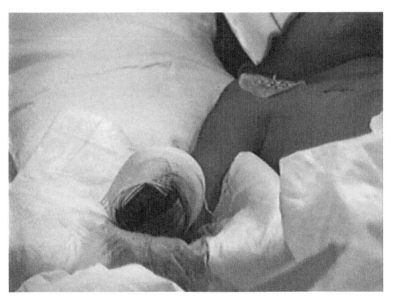

Wounded boy, Mostar, 1994.

Sandbags at the Malaysian UN Base at Konjic, early 1995.

Ruins of Mostar, early 1995.

On the road.

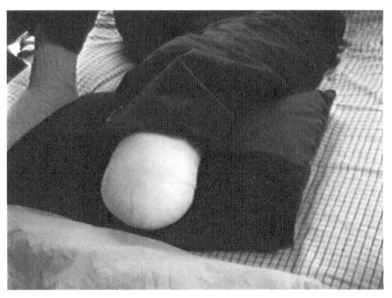

Amputee, Banovici, 1995.

Refugee cooking in field, northern Bosnia, autumn 1995.

Refugees in field, northern Bosnia, autumn 1995.

Road through the forests and mountains, central Bosnia.

Sarajevo cat, early 1996.

Bosnian Croat soldiers in Tomislavgrad.

British UN base at Vitez, early 1994.

Pakistani UN soldiers, northern Bosnia, early 1995.

Ruins of Mostar.

The author playing pool in Dutch UN base near Tuzla, early 1995. Tony watching.

Canadian UN troops at UN HQ, Kiseljak.

Abandoned tank near Donji Vakuf, early 1996.

Temporary bridge replacing Mostar's Stari Most, early 1994.

Stretchers outside Bugojno hospital, autumn 1994.

Damaged kettle, Mostar.

Building housing refugees in Travnik in 1994.

Unloading in the snow in Tuzla, early 1995.

35

DALMACIJA

In the war films
that flicker on the multiplex screens
something's always happening.
Well you've got to keep
the audience's attention.

People run,
people scream,
buildings explode,
aircraft crash.

All those happen
in real wars, of course,
but not in all places
and not all the time.

Somebody said they built
the Hotel Dalmacija for
the Sarajevo Winter Olympics,
a temple of 80s steel and glass chic.

A bit shabby by 1995
but still with a lovely sun terrace
and a view of the mountains
about 30km from Sarajevo.

The tourists are gone
and in their place
live the blue-hatted staff
of a UN HQ.

They're all busy
but if you're passing through
with your truck
and you have an excuse
to pass a lazy morning,
perfect place to do so.

Waiting for paperwork?
Need some spares for the lorry?
Meeting someone?
Then relish the joys of Kiseljak's
Hotel Dalmacija.

For breakfast choose from
French UN continental,
Canadian UN waffles and syrup,
Malaysian UN curry and cold chips,
or British UN, good old full English.

Then take tea
from massive British army tea urns
on the sun terrace.
Fill up as many times as you like.

Use the phone boxes
to phone a loved one in Britain
and feel for a few minutes
a connection across Europe
to a place of peace and normality.

Then more tea on the terrace
and watch the UN helicopters
land and take off
while the Canadians work on their
armoured cars in the park below.

And slowly,
like an approaching war,
the snow clouds advance
down the hill towards you,
until you can see individual flakes,
and the crystals settle on your skin.

GORGE

Gorge, gorge,
gorgeous gorge.
Who'd ever heard
of the Neretva Gorge
before the war?
Not many people
in Britain, that's for sure.
Not me, though I'd
travelled in Yugoslavia.

But it was here,
long before humankind,
(not always kind)
and maybe it'll be here
long mega-centuries after.
Massive, silent, prompting
almost slack-jawed awe.

Oh the war has touched it.
Bridges, broken, blown,
megalithic themselves,
jut at bizarre angles,
or reach to nowhere,
and the clatter, clatter
pontoon bridge
or bailey bridge
is clamped in their place.

But it's like a war of ants.
The gorge looks down on it,
rock eyes firm closed,
unmoved, unnoticing,
and, if we're frank,
uncaring too.
Perhaps though
the blue Neretva cares,
it would be nice to think.

It is not chained in place
like the gorge but flows free
from the mountains
down towards Mostar
onto a plain sunny
but burned, bruised and blackened,
where the diesel drone of the truck
matches the sight and sight, sight
of killed home after killed home.

GUN CREW

The old Bedford,
painted white on the outside,
still old army green on the inside,
rattles and bangs over a rock.
Coffee-brown water swirls
in the holes torn in the road surface,
and splashes up,
clinging like lost hands at the truck,
redecorating its white
Jackson Pollock-splashed brown.

To our left and right
house after house,
burned black rafters
open to the sky,
many walls still strangely white
except where the fire from windows
has scorched them,
and gardens still strangely neat.
No old, weed-decorated
ruins are these.
Chimneys, now lonely

bereft of their embracing roof,
stand sentinel over the desolation.
Ahead of us on the road,
where it weaves between
not long abandoned orchards,
a glimpse on the road,
a glimpse that
as we slowly catch up
metamorphizes into a bulldozer
trailing a gun
and carrying its crew.
The ceasefire is holding for now
and they are leaving
the frontline these lads.
Three men perch precariously
between the gun carriage
and the bulldozer,
two more sit
out of mud range
on the rear of the bulldozer,
clad in any different part
of camouflage clothing
they could lay hands on,
civilian jerseys
showing jaunty colours beneath.
These lads
they're not sad
to leave the carnage
and rubble-strewn chaos
of Gornji Vakuf,
not sad at all.
In fact they seem bloody delighted.
As we come up close behind,
two of them, older these,
late 30s, 40s maybe even
grin and wave

while the young one,
the joker of the pack,
seated high on the bulldozer,
AK hung around his neck,
sticks his right hand up
in triumph
and does a gleeful
high kick with his right leg,
like a booted can-can dancer,
face split
by a shout of joy.
And then they're gone,
the youngest one still cheering.
The road forks and
we go right,
past the checkpoint,
up the hill on the long grind
to Vitez and Travnik.
They go left,
to where? To what?
The side war
between Croats and Bosniaks
may be over (may be)
the war with the Serbs goes on.

GORNJI VAKUF

The lamp-post is
a thing almost of strange beauty,
something that belongs perhaps
in a plush West End art gallery,
or fine white-walled museum.
Transformed by the
frontline's flying metal
from solid pillar to a
delicate lace-like structure,
fingers of twisted metal
reaching across the air
to each other,
the post's skin pierced
time and time again
by bullets and shells.
Hard to believe almost
that it still has
the strength to stand.
And in that sense
it stands for the
battered town itself.
Nearby somebody
has sprayed on a
wall pocked by bullets
a black figure of death,
scythe over shoulder,
and the word
ZOMBI next to it.
Nearby a UN team
explodes
an abandoned
rifle grenade.

I jump a little
and swear.

TRAVNIK

'Any time is
shelling Travnik,
any time.'
He'd come from Sarajevo
and now he was
'some kind of refugee'
in Travnik.
His teenage face was
thin with stress
and hunger,
the coming moustache
and beard throwing
his almost hollow cheeks
into chiselled relief.
He sat tensed and
spoke of the enemy,
two kilometres distant
and he spoke of the shells
that fell on Travnik,
how they expected
them now any time,
how they feared the shells
and took to the shelters
when the shells fell,
how one his friends
fifteen years old
who before had played
football and karate,
before 'had a life',
had been closer
to the shell than him
and now the friend
just sat
and watched TV
and how the shells
took the young lives

of two of his other friends
and how another shell
killed many people
in one house.
And he had a message
for British people,
the people of Britainy
he called them,
speaking a language
not his own,
'Don't ever try
to make any war.'
Something was odd
about him
and then I realised
what it was.
Almost no smiles,
a teenager
who didn't smile
or grin any more,
either in happiness
or embarrassment.

The gun was silent, distant
but the bullet spoke,
a high sibilance
shouting sharply
in Mostar's
warm Autumn air.
Such a small thing.

Through slow milliseconds
the size of its
near impact
coldly licked our cheeks
sending a twinge
up neck
and down neurone.

In the frozen fraction
before we ran,
you had said,
with your customary eloquence,
'Ere, come on…'
I interrupted,
with my usual perspicacity,
'Fucking hell,
that was a bullet'.

YELLOW JERSEY

She was dancing with the lens,
the happiest-looking little girl
that you ever saw,
maybe 9 or 10 years old,
her whole face
one big smiling
chip-toothed gap-toothed mouth
with big, big laughing eyes,
a chunky hair-band
keeping her brown hair
well clear of that sunny face,
one little green earring
jumping as she twisted with glee,
her jersey bright and yellow.
But that was Mostar in 1994,
a few days into the ceasefire,
a few days since the siege ended,
and her face was thin
and the wall behind her
was pocked by shell splinters.
And further up the street
where the UN's Spanish battalion
had parked their big white APCs,
safe-ish under cover
and behind sandbag walls,
other kids crawled in glee
over the sloping white metal
obscuring the big black letters
U and N with their bodies.
The kids have been through hell,
but will they ever see heaven?

'TATA!'

He couldn't see his father any longer
so he had to call.
A fly idly flicked across his bandaged face,
his skin pockmarked with grenade splinters
like premature acne.

'Tata!'

Would he see again?
Eight maybe going on ten,
not enough years in which to absorb
a lifetime's looking,
to file a spectrum for a shadow future.

'Tata!'

He reached with his voice.
He could no longer
reach with his right hand,
taken by the explosion
that amputated his dreams.

BONEZONE

The skeletons
of a thousand homes
and more and more
lie naked,
ribs open to the
cold sky,
eye sockets black,
glass long gone,
mouths grinning wide.
Come on in.
It's death inside.

SIGNS

You might long
for something a little cheerier,
like 'Roadworks, Long Queues Likely'
or even 'M25 Closed, Long Delays'
when, in reality,
road signs flashing past
your (soft-skinned) truck
and (soft-skinned) you
carry captions like
'Danger!
No UN soft skin vehicle
beyond this point
without escort.
We care for your security'
or something simpler like just
'Attention Snipers next 2 Km'.

Some say it's easier
to be brave
when you're young.
Easier to risk your life
before you've yet
learned fully to love it,
to value its richness,
its joy, its sadness,
its heartaching beauty,
and the children,
loves, home places
that it may bring.

Maybe.
But when we're old
and with just a few days,
weeks, months, years
left to live,
we will drive
at 15mph
and hang onto the last
grey scraps of life
with all the passion
we once used
in flaunting our young lives
and trying to change
the world a bit
(and we will still
think of those
who grew not old).

WEATHER

Why do wars seem so often
born in hot sunshine,
with smiling, excited faces
bright colours
and summer clothes
but ending in grey mist,
and rain and mud,
cold, drab, weary frowns?

The heat of August 1914,
with ladies balancing
broad-brimmed summer hats,
turned to the muddy slog
of November 1918.
The sun of September 1939,
with women flashing deco smiles
became the cold, firm-jawed
early months of 1945.
The summer of Croatia 1991,
with women grinning
and throwing victory signs,
ended in the Balkan sleet
of 1995's late Autumn.

Perhaps statistics and research
will say that it's not true.
Maybe it is just coincidence
or perhaps it's just
the 'fighting season'
and all that,
or maybe the weather
is just a mental metaphor
for early hope
turned to numb exhaustion
(even for the victors).

Or perhaps
the weather is
sending us a message.
'Looking sunny and bright,
at the start, but all that
heat and hate developing fast,
and then the outlook
turns very, very nasty,
with a depression sweeping in
bringing showers of metal
and mass death later.
And that's the forecast.
Thanks for listening.
Good night.'

Nightmare Job

It's true that
the world holds
many crap jobs.
Yours, O reader unknown,
may be one of them.

But spare a brief thought
for anybody
running a
petrol station
within range of
enemy artillery.

Yep.

This one's got
so many sandbags and
so much wood
round the kiosk
that you can't actually
see the kiosk
any more.
Of course,
even in a war
loads of people
still need petrol,
so maybe
they make
really good money.

But still…

CAR

The car had been
a little over-ambitious
cornering on
Route Triangle,
mud and rock
logging track
turned lifeline
to central Bosnia.
It lay on its side
wheels now uselessly
gripping the air.
Shouldn't laugh really.
Wouldn't, in Britain.
Somebody could have
been injured inside.
But, hey, it's a war.

KETTLE

Somebody killed the kettle,
its cheap metal form
disembowelled by
rather more expensive metal
slashing through at high speed,
peeling it open and laying bare
its innards.
Now it lies inert,
splayed amidst the war rubble.
The kettle's dead.
Hope its owners aren't.

The four players
hunch over their cards
intent on nothing
but the fan of rectangles
in their hands,
sorting, analysing, plotting.
Suddenly one leans in
quick to strike
depositing a card.
But the others
hardly seem to notice.
The game has only just begun
and no victor
will claim his laurels
yet awhile.
It is almost like
a scene from art,
Hogarth perhaps,
but this is no London salon.
Instead, the four players
ignoring the dead
buildings around them,
sit, in camouflage
rather than peacock silks
atop a big dirty white UN APC
its tracks sunk deep
in the middle of glutinous mud
the whole sunk deep
in the middle of Bosnia,
in the middle of the war.

Kids

In the third year of the war,
in a tired town in central Bosnia,
with the start of the war long gone
and the end unseeable,
two small boys stare
at me in my truck
while we wait for other trucks.
I grin idly and wave at them.
They smile, shy and awkward.
Best friends perhaps?
They seem about the same age,
maybe 8 or 9.
Or brothers perhaps?
They are dressed so alike,
in bright but fading winter jackets
old jeans and muddy boots
(mud everywhere this time of year).
A real war's going on around them,
people dying, villages and towns dying
but boys will be boys.
The slightly taller kid
carries a wooden toy Kalashnikov.
It has been carefully made
and has good detail.
Well he's seen enough of
the real type to know
if his doesn't look right.
But the bigger kid's
looking at the smaller kid.
As am I.
No wooden AK for the little one.
He has a real olive-green,
scratched metal, cold steel,
(unloaded I hope)
grenade launcher.
It's almost as tall as him.

The kid smiles and
raises the sights
raises the (empty I think)
tube on his shoulder
and still smiling shyly
aims the launcher at us,
as if at a friend.

KIT KID

I was born in the 1960s,
was a kid in the 1970s,
fed on a diet of
World War 2 films
and Airfix kits,
rushing to finish
gluing them
so I could admire
the finished tank,
leaning down
in front of it
and squinting up
to make it look big,
before turning its turret
(if the glue hadn't got
where it shouldn't)
slowly and menacingly.
Sometimes if I was
feeling artistic
I'd make a diorama
(think that's what
they called it,

a nice, long,
technical word)
of a dead tank,
track half ripped off,
turret at an angle.
Never thought then
I'd be in Bosnia now,
seeing the same
tanks for real.
A T-34 abandoned
by the roadside
snow-trimmed
turret still turned
in the wrong direction.
A World War 2
US tank destroyer,
once supplied to
Tito's army
broken track
curling snake-like
eating into the mud,
engine covers gaping,
dead tank,
pushed without ceremony
from the road,
in retreat.
Metal, not plastic,
last gasp of Europe's
bloody 20th century.

BUTTERFLY

Yes it's all crap the war,
what with all that death
and all those lungfuls of hate,
where looks can kill
but even more so shells,
and what's lacking is a butterfly.

'Cos what you want is a butterfly,
spreading its wings over the carnage,
dodging the shells,
its fragility defying death,
a life the opposite of war,
that doesn't look like it could hate.

SIXTY

The young doctor
outside the small hospital
was handsome,
firm jawed
and lightly tanned.
He could almost have been
starring in a US hospital drama
instead of standing
in the middle of a war.

He seemed tense.
It was very dangerous
around there, he said,
with a lot of firing.
Raiders had attacked
not far distant.

The late summer sunlight
glowed warm but
his words were cold.

'We had sixty deaths' he said.
Within two hours
they had to deal with
thirty injured he said.

Even he gave the impression of
being a little surprised
though he must have seen a lot.

Sixty deaths.
A drop in the blood-red ocean of war.
But a big one.

RAKIJA

Rakija liquor you give me.
The coffee is dark
and bitter as death,
like a gun-barrel
that stares from
the saucer.

Around,
Autumn smoulders
lairily on the hills,
frazzling the senses,
nature with no restraint.
It will be weeks before
December's firemen
dowse the blaze.

In the valley
man has helped
Autumn's decoration.
the town's burning shops
spit hatred into the streets
and black leaves fall gently.

You give me coffee and rakija.
The rakija smells a bit like
petrol and smoke,
and it burns,
cauterising for a while
the jagged holes
in our mind.

The rain fell in no-man's land,
tip tap, tip tip tap,
irregularly regular
(like single shots from an automatic AK)
wounding leaves,
peppering the damp hillside.

The refugees
stood or sat or leant
but all waited wet chilled
in an abandoned petrol station,
no fuel, no destination,
the collective noun for desperation
robbed of life
and given existence.

Out of the swirling mist
their bright winter clothing
lunged at our vision,
all in silence
to ears deafened
by the whine
of diesel.